DATE			

Celebrating the Peoples and Civilizations of Southeast Asia™

THE PEOPLE OF
THAILAND

Dolly Brittan

The Rosen Publishing Group's
PowerKids Press™
New York

Published in 1997 by The Rosen Publishing Group, Inc.
29 East 21st Street, New York, NY 10010

First Edition

Book Design: Danielle Primiceri

Photo Credits: Cover © Bobbe Wolf/Chicago/International Stock; p. 4 © Roger Markham-Smith/ International Stock; p. 7, 20 (bottom) © Chad Ehlers/International Stock; pp. 8, 11, 19, 20 (top and middle) © Cliff Hollenbeck/International Stock; p. 12 © Robert C. Russell/International Stock; p. 15 © Orion/International Stock; p. 16 © Roberto Arakaki/International Stock; p. 20 (background) © Chang Mia/International Stock.

Brittan, Dolly.
    The people of Thailand / Dolly Brittan.
        p.   cm. (Celebrating the peoples and civilizations of Southeast Asia)
    Summary: Introduces the culture, religion, landscape, and beliefs of the Thai people of Thailand.
    ISBN 0-8239-5126-X
    1. Thailand—Juvenile literature. [1. Thailand.] I. Title. II. Series.
    DS563.5.B75 1996
    959.3—dc21
                                       96-47347
                                          CIP
                                           AC

Manufactured in the United States of America

Contents

A Land Called Thailand   5

The National Symbol   6

The Culture   9

The Language   10

Farming   13

Shopping   14

Religion   17

Thai Dancing   18

Art and Craft   21

Old and New   22

Glossary   23

Index   24

MYANMAR

LAOS

THAILAND

Bangkok

CAMBODIA

VIETNAM

South China
Sea

A Land Called Thailand

Thailand (TY-land) is a very old country in Southeast Asia. It was once called **Siam** (sy-AM). The **Thai** (TY) people have their own name for Thailand: **Muang Thai** (moo-ANG TY), which means "The Land of the Free."

The capital city of Thailand is **Bangkok** (BANG-kok). The area around Bangkok, where most Thai people live, is called the Central Plain. About half of Thailand has forests of bamboo, palm trees, and many kinds of ferns. Much of the rest of the land is covered by farms, grassland, and swamps.

Although much of Thailand is covered with forests and farmland, it has cities such as Bangkok.

The National Symbol

Many animals live in Thailand's forests. Tigers and leopards roam the jungle. Elephants are tamed and trained to haul logs. The elephant is Thailand's national **symbol** (SIM-bul). Thailand also has rhinoceroses, crocodiles, monkeys, and apes.

The most famous animal from Thailand is the Siamese cat, with its blue eyes. The Thai say that long ago these smart cats kept Thai **temples** (TEM-pulz) safe from harm.

It can be difficult to drive a truck through the forest to carry logs to town. It is easier to have an elephant haul logs through the forest. ▶

The Culture

Thai **culture** (KUL-cher) is at least 1,500 years old. In the past, the Thai people were **influenced** (IN-flu-enst) by their neighbors, the Indians and the Chinese.

The Thai people celebrate many festivals and ceremonies. During the Loy Krathong festival, people float banana leaves decorated with candles in rivers and canals to honor the water spirits.

The Thai believe that it is important to be friendly, to speak softly, and to help each other.

There are many festivals and celebrations in Thailand.

The Language

The Thai language is in some ways like Chinese. It is made up of short words. And changing the tone of a word changes its meaning. The same word spoken in different tones can mean "dog," or "horse," or "to come."

The English alphabet has 26 letters. But the Thai language has 76 **consonants** (KON-suh-nints) and **vowel** (VOWL) sounds. The Thai alphabet was invented 800 years ago by King Rama Kamheng. His alphabet is still used today.

Although the language may sound a little different, Thai children today use the same alphabet that Thai children used hundreds of years ago. ▶

Farming

Experts believe that the first human farmers might have lived in Thailand. Scientists have found very old metal tools and the world's oldest plant seeds in Thailand.

Rice is grown in Thailand. It is a favorite food of many Thai people. Growing rice is hard work, but the soil and weather in Thailand is just right for rice. Thailand grows so much rice that it has plenty to sell to other countries and still has enough to feed its own people.

◀ *Rice farmers work long, hard days. They start early in the morning and finish just before dark.*

Shopping

Rather than shopping in crowded stores, some Thai people buy food and other things they need from street **vendors** (VEN-derz).

Some parts of Bangkok are built along the banks of the river **Chao Phrya** (CHOW PRA-ja). Instead of streets, there are **canals** (kah-NALZ) filled with water. These canals are called ***klongs*** (KLONGS) in Thai. People travel on the *klongs* by boat. And vendors sell goods from boats in these areas.

Some Thai people shop in stores. Others like to buy food from vendors in the boats that fill the canals. ▶

Religion

The Thai religion is **Buddhism** (BOOD-ism). Buddhism is a religion that began in India. **Buddha** (BOO-dah) was the holy man and teacher who started Buddhism. *Wat* (WAT) is the Thai word for temple. There are 27,000 Buddhist temples in Thailand.

Buddhist priests live in **monasteries** (MON-ah-stayr-ees). Most Thai boys spend three months a year in a monastery. They study Buddhism there. The boys wear orange robes and sandals and shave off all the hair on their face and heads.

Some boys decide to stay at a monastery and study Buddhism for many years.

Thai Dancing

Girls learn how to dance gracefully as soon as they start school. Dancers wear beautiful costumes and fancy headdresses. They also wear colorful jewelry.

Each Thai dance tells a story. Every dance movement shows a feeling. Placing one hand on the heart means "love."

Some dancers wear long, gold tips on the ends of their fingers. This makes the movements of their hands easier to see. ▶

Art and Craft

The Thai are famous for their beautiful jewelry and **sculptures** (SKULP-cherz). Some people say that Thailand has more statues of Buddha than it has people! This is not really true. But there are thousands of sculptures of Buddha in all shapes and sizes. Many are made of metal and some are covered in gold.

Many Thai people weave silk cloth. Some people still make the shiny silk cloth by hand on **looms** (LOOMZ). Sometimes metal threads are put into the cloth to make it sparkle.

◀ *Although most silk cloth is now made by machines, some Thai people still weave it by hand on looms.*

Old and New

In the last 30 years, there have been many changes in Thailand. The new buildings, clothes, and cars look like those in the United States. But the Thai culture is still very strong. People still make and fly beautiful Thai kites. Kites are made by stretching heavy paper over a bamboo frame. People paint beautiful designs on their kites. Kite fighting is still a popular sport. People try to knock other kites out of the sky by flying their kites into other kites. The people of Thailand are bringing together the culture of the past and the future.

Glossary

Bangkok (BANG-kok) The capital of Thailand.
Buddha (BOO-dah) The holy teacher who started Buddhism.
Buddhism (BOOD-ism) The Thai religion.
canal (kah-NAL) Waterways for travel.
Chao Phrya (CHOW PRA-ja) A river in Bangkok.
consonant (KON-suh-nint) A sound that forms part of a word.
culture (KUL-cher) The customs, art, and beliefs of a people.
influence (IN-flu-ents) The effect a person or thing has on another.
klong (KLONG) The Thai word for canal.
loom (LOOM) A tool used to weave fabric.
monastery (MON-ah-stayr-ee) A place where monks live.
Muang Thai (moo-ANG TY) Thai for "the land of the free."
sculpture (SKULP-cher) The art of carving or molding figures.
Siam (sy-AM) The old name for Thailand.
symbol (SIM-bul) A thing that represents something else.
temple (TEM-pul) A place of worship.
Thai (TY) The people of Thailand.
Thailand (TY-land) A country in Southeast Asia.
vendor (VEN-der) A person who sells something.
vowel (VOWL) A soft sounding letter.
wat (WAT) The Thai word for temple.

23

Index

A
animals, 6
Asia, 5

B
Bangkok, 5
Buddha, 21
Buddhism, 17

C
canals, 14
cats, Siamese, 6
Chao Phrya, 14
China and the
        Chinese, 9, 10
culture, 9

D
dancing, 18

E
elephants, 6

F
farming, 13
festivals, 9
forests, 5, 6

I
India and Indians, 9

K
Kamheng, King
        Rama, 10

L
language, 10

M
monasteries, 17

R
religion, 17
rice, 13

S
sculptures, 21
shopping, 14
Southeast Asia, 5

T
temples, 6, 17

W
weaving, 21